Prok

Prok
first published 2003 by
Scirocco Drama
An imprint of J. Gordon Shillingford Publishing Inc.
©2002 Brian Drader

Scirocco Drama Series Editor: Glenda MacFarlane
Cover Art by Guppy Design
Cover Design by Doowah Design Inc.
Author photo by Kathy Clune
Printed and bound in Canada

Published with the financial assistance of The Canada Council for the Arts
and the Manitoba Arts Council.

Production enquiries should be addressed to:
Playwrights Union of Canada
54 Wolseley Street, 2nd Floor
Toronto, ON M5T 1A5

Canadian Cataloguing in Publication Data

Drader, Brian, 1960–
    Prok/Brian Drader.

A play.
ISBN 1-896239-97-8
    I. Title.
PS8557.R2734P76 2002   C812'.54   C2002-906006-0
PR9199.3.D725P76 2003

J. Gordon Shillingford Publishing
P.O. Box 86, 905 Corydon Avenue, Winnipeg, MB Canada R3M 3S3

PROK

BRIAN DRADER

Acknowledgements

The playwright wishes to acknowledge and thank Iris Turcott for her ongoing and invaluable dramaturgical support, and Maureen LaBonte, Margo Charlton, Janet Michael, Anne George, and Kathy Clune for their advice and feedback.

The playwright also wishes to acknowledge and thank James H. Jones, whose biography *Alfred C. Kinsey, A Public/Private Life*, was central to his research.

Written with the assistance of the Manitoba Arts Council and The National Theatre School of Canada.

Brian Drader

Brian is an actor and writer who makes his home in Winnipeg, Manitoba.

In addition to *Prok*, his writing credits include *The Norbals* (winner of the Herman Voaden National Playwriting Competition, and also published by Scirocco Drama), *S*it* (a play for teens), *The Fruit Machine*, and *Tucktuck*. Two early plays, *Mind of the Iguana* and *Easter Eggs*, were both co-written with Stephen McIntyre. Another play, *Bubba and the Peter Eater*, was a finalist in the Theatre BC National Playwriting Competition in 1996, and his short film, *Iris and Nathan*, won the National Screen Institute Drama Prize in 1995.

As an actor, he has over 70 stage credits and numerous television and film credits.

Production Credits

Prok was originally produced by Theatre Projects Manitoba, Winnipeg, and premiered on November 15, 2001, with the following cast:

KINSEY .... Richard Hurst
CLARA .... Patricia Hunter
MR.X .... Arne McPherson

Directed by Margo Charlton
Set and Costume Design by Grant Guy
Sound Design by Marilyn Lerner
Lighting Design by Dean Cowison
Stage Manager: Sara Lawson

A huge thank you to TPM, and the artistic and technical team of this production for their assistance in the development of the play.

Cast

Actor 1   Clara Kinsey, at all ages

Actor 2   Alfred C. Kinsey, at all ages

Actor 3   Mr. X, who plays the characters of Victor, David, Arnold Wolfe, Dr. Medley, the Beat Poet, and Mr. Lawrence.

Notes on Design

The following design notes are a suggestion; the visual landscape the playwright used in creating the piece. The design is open to interpretation.

Act I   A strong visual sense of a forest, a wilderness, giving over to cultivated flower gardens. The gardens, although robust, seem to be a work-in-progress. It isn't clear whether the garden is claiming space from the forest or the forest is reclaiming space from the garden. The sound of insects and birds abound, comforting, a hot summer afternoon, eventually giving over to the sound of insects interspersed with distant, indistinct human sounds that might be sex, or discomfort.

Act II   A strong visual sense of a garden long ago lost to neglect, twisted, dead plants, thick and gloomy. Weeds poke through the rotting undergrowth. The forest is moving in, taking over everything. There is a feeling of danger; we get the sense that there may be wild animals lurking in the undergrowth just beyond. The sound of insects takes over, stands alone, a virulent plague, a disease, out of control.

All playing areas could be suggested in and around the garden and forest with lighting and minimal properties.

The slides/images noted in the text are Kinsey's lecture and research slides, although they don't always appear in that context. They could be used literally i.e. a projector operated by the actors onstage. In the TPM production, Mr. X's letter in Act I was recorded and played over the action taking place on stage. It was very effective.

A forward slash (/) in the text indicates overlapping dialogue.

Act I

Gall Wasps in the Garden of Eden

Sound of birds and insects, comforting, a hot and sunny spring day.

CLARA KINSEY is sitting in a rocker. She is a small, pretty woman, dressed plainly, almost masculinely. She has short, straight hair, no make-up.

A small storage crate sits beside her rocker. CLARA is poking through it. She picks up a flint, examines it, rolling it over in her hand.

She takes in the audience.

CLARA: In the beginning...

ALFRED C. KINSEY is found, crouching over a tiny bunch of twigs, in a forest clearing. He is a tall, good-looking man, vigorous and fit. He is building a fire, using a flint, identical to the one CLARA holds.

CLARA notices him, just a slight distraction at first, a shadow, but gradually she takes him in, remembering. She absent-mindedly drops the flint she still has in her hand.

KINSEY hears something—perhaps a bird or a rabbit in the dense, lush undergrowth beyond. He reacts as an animal would, fully alert, aware, senses heightened. He looks for the source of the sound, can't see anything, and dismisses it, returning to his task.

Sparks.

CLARA approaches him.

CLARA: Hello Professor Kinsey.

KINSEY: Hmm? Can I help you?

CLARA: I was just taking a little stroll. Why aren't you with
            the others?

KINSEY: Do I know you? Are you one of mine?

CLARA: Your...

KINSEY: Students.

CLARA: Oh. No. I'm a Chemistry major. Clara MacMillan.

            KINSEY strikes his flint. Sparks.

KINSEY: I didn't know students were invited. I thought it
            was a Faculty outing.

CLARA: I asked Professor Scott if I could come along. I'm
            taking his ornithology course. I thought it might be
            a good chance to do some field work.

KINSEY: Good for you. I'm quite a bird enthusiast myself.

CLARA: Professor Scott tells me you used to lecture on the
            subject.

KINSEY: Yes.

            KINSEY continues to work his flint.

CLARA: I have matches, if you'd like.

KINSEY: No need.

            *KINSEY works a spark inside a small clump of dried
            grass, nursing it.*

CLARA: I saw a short billed linnet earlier, down by the lake.

KINSEY: The passeres family. What are the traits of a passerine?

CLARA: Singing birds that perch.

KINSEY: Very good. William must be pleased with you.

CLARA: William?

KINSEY: Professor Scott.

CLARA: Oh. Of course. I forget sometimes that they have first names.

               I'm sorry. You're one of they. Them. It's just…you're so much younger than…sorry. It's really quite rude of me to be barging in on you like this. Well. Barging in. It's not as if this is your bedroom. Kitchen, your kitchen, rather. It's the outdoors, and you can't really barge 'in' to the 'out' doors, can you?

               KINSEY hasn't been listening. He's managed to get a small flame going.

               But it's still rather forward of me. I do apologize.

               Professor Kinsey?

KINSEY: Hmm? Yes?

CLARA: Can I give you a hand with anything?

KINSEY: No, I'm fine. Thank you.

CLARA: Are you going to be joining the others for lunch? I think they're doing fish.

KINSEY: I'm going down to the lake to catch my own.

CLARA: Oh, really? I love fishing.

               Silence. KINSEY works his flame.

               Well. I suppose I should be heading back. I do hope

we'll run into each other again soon. I'm planning on taking your taxonomy course next semester.

KINSEY: Good. Very Good.

CLARA: Yes. Well. I'm off. *(CLARA begins to leave, stops.)* Can I come fishing with you?

KINSEY: Pardon?

CLARA: I've decided I'm going to go fishing with you. I hope you don't mind.

KINSEY: I suppose not. Do you know how?

CLARA: Yes.

KINSEY: Good. Very good then. Find us a couple of good pickerel rods. A maple switch is best. It's got the right give.

> *KINSEY returns to his fire tending, and CLARA goes back to her rocker. A 1920s style record player sits nearby. She makes her way over to it, and puts on a record, one of KINSEY's favourite classical piano pieces, Greig or Chopin or Beethoven. She listens to the music for a moment. It underscores the following.*

CLARA: In the beginning…

> *She takes in the audience, on her own time. She's in no particular hurry.*

I confess. I didn't wrangle an invitation to the Zoology Department picnic to catch up on my bird watching. I was stalking him, thank you very much. Don't knock it. It worked. Two months after we met, he asked me to marry him.

For Christmas that year, as an engagement present, he gave me a compass, a hunting knife, and a pair of Clara Bass hiking boots. For an engagement present. That was his idea of romance.

And then for our honeymoon, we went on a gorgeous three week camping trip through the White Mountains of New England. Of course, you appreciate a good pair of hiking boots more than just about anything on a three week camping trip, and they soon came to symbolize the very epitome of romance; Prok's way of making sure that I was comfortable, that I was taken care of.

They lasted me a good ten years, those boots, and then I retired them. Put them away with my wedding dress.

The sound of birds and insects.

It's a sunny day in late spring. KINSEY is collecting gall wasp nests from the branches of trees. It is precise and focused work. He is consumed by it.

CLARA watches him.

Prok.

He called me Mac, short for MacMillian. I liked it, having a boy's name. Mac. Had a good bite to it. Sounded right, coming from him.

Prok. Sounds like something a chicken would say. Prok prok prok prok prok prok. It never sounded like that when he was alive. Prok. *(Calling to him.)* Prok! Prok!

KINSEY: Over here.

CLARA: *(She approaches.)* What are you doing?

KINSEY: Collecting samples.

CLARA: You said you'd be back by six. I had supper ready. I've been beating my way through the bush for over an hour looking for you.

KINSEY: Sorry. I must have lost track of time.

CLARA: For heaven's sake, Al, it's our honeymoon. Surely your precious bugs can wait.

KINSEY: They're gall wasps / of the Genus Cynips...

CLARA: / of the Genus Cynips, I know. But when supper has been waiting for over an hour their classification broadens considerably. They are bugs.

KINSEY: Come here. I want to show you something.

CLARA: What.

                CLARA goes to him. He puts his arm around her, bringing her in close, showing her the galls on the tree branches.

KINSEY: Every branch of every tree, every single one is covered with galls. The entire stand is like this. It's extraordinary. I've never seen anything quite like it.

                Why don't you join me? Supper can wait until the sun goes down.

CLARA: It's already ruined, I don't suppose it'll make any difference now.

KINSEY: Here. You can record.

                He hands her a clipboard, and they begin collecting, him with his tweezers and scalpel, her with pencil and paper.

                It's an excellent time of year to collect. Most of the eggs have hatched. The galls are abandoned. I'll have over 10,000 by the end of the summer. That's an undeniable sample size.

                Casually looking at CLARA's notes.

                You can mark this as a 22-year-old. An oak.

CLARA: I know what kind of tree it is, Al.

KINSEY: Sorry.

            They collect and record.

            Victor Harding is going to assist me with the cataloguing, as part of his doctorate.

CLARA: Do I know him?

KINSEY: One of my Entomology students from last semester. He sat at our table at the year end dinner. His field work impresses me. Very thorough. He chose his own dissertation. He's going to focus on beetles of the family Staphylinidae. Could be valuable work.

CLARA: You have nice shoulders.

KINSEY: Pardon?

CLARA: Your shoulders. I can see the muscles move when you reach.

KINSEY: Oh. Well. I haven't gotten a burn or anything, have I?

CLARA: No.

KINSEY: That's good.

            KINSEY goes back to his collecting.

            I love being out here. Always have. Since my scouting days. Did I ever tell you I was one of the first scouts to acheive the rank of Eagle? All my badges were for outdoor activities.

CLARA: You know I'm a virgin.

            Silence.

KINSEY: Yes. I assumed.

CLARA: Are you?

KINSEY: Yes.

CLARA: Will you be patient with me?

KINSEY: I should hope that we'll both be patient.

            Silence.

CLARA: It's going to be a beautiful sunset, I think.

KINSEY: Yes.

            Sound of insects and birds, comforting.

            CLARA returns to her rocker, leaving KINSEY to continue collecting. She addresses the audience.

CLARA: Did you know that swans are the only animal, other than humans, in which the female of the species has an orgasm? Or at least it's the only species in which the orgasm of the female is similar enough to ours that we can recognize it for what it is. There might be earth shaking, window rattling female orgasms happening all around us on a physiological plane that we haven't even begun to understand…

            There's something about that—the idea that we're surrounded by little female sexual explosions, insects and birds and lions and otters and all manner of womanly beast popping off in ways we couldn't possibly comprehend—there's something about that idea I find oddly comforting.

            She takes in KINSEY, watching him.

            I wonder what happened to those two sweet innocent things, fumbling in the dark, so anxious and unable to please each other. It's as if I'm not connected to them anymore, as if they were two people I read about in a book, or saw in a movie or a play…

*KINSEY gets up and goes over to the record player.
He selects a record, puts it on the turntable. CLARA
joins him, standing to one side, smiling, the hostess.*

*MR. X is found, sitting off to the side, attentive,
waiting, one of KINSEY's guests.*

KINSEY: Settle please. Excuse me, we're ready to begin...

The sound of birds and insects fades to silence.

Thank you. Now, this is a lovely little piece by
Chopin. His Waltz in D Flat. The story concerning
the playing of this particular waltz in a minute—
thus its nickname, 'the minute waltz'—is
apocryphal, really. To do so would make utter
nonsense of this delightful miniature. Its proper
playing time is actually one minute and forty four
seconds. Listen.

*He places the needle, and the waltz begins to play.
He stands back and watches the audience. CLARA
continues to stand and smile.*

*KINSEY observes, and CLARA smiles. The music
begins to skip.*

*The skipping record fades to silence, as CLARA
returns to her rocker, and KINSEY approaches MR.
X.*

KINSEY: Did you see how it held my guests? Particularly the
women. It's as if it doesn't want you to breathe, but
to simply lift and turn, suspended, the perfect
waltz. The man was a genius.

MR. X: I want to thank you again for inviting me this
evening. It's quite an honour, to be asked to one of
your infamous musicales.

KINSEY: The honour is entirely mine, Victor. I'm glad you
could come.

MR. X: I've never really listened to much classical music. I'm a bit of a jazz man myself.

KINSEY: I'll cure you of that vile sickness soon enough. You should have a browse through my records. I believe it's the largest classical collection in the mid-west.

MR. X: Perhaps another time, Professor Kinsey. I'm sure I've overstayed my welcome. Everyone else left ages ago.

KINSEY: You can call me Prok, if you'd like.

MR. X: ...pardon me?

KINSEY: I was told that you were the one who started it. It's certainly caught on with the student body. Clara's even taken to it. You should stand up and claim ownership before it gets away from you.

MR. X: I'm sorry. It's short for / Professor and...

KINSEY: / Professor and Kinsey, yes, I gathered that.

MR. X: I didn't mean it critically. I made it up as a kind of shorthand. I refer to you often.

KINSEY: Really.

MR. X: You're the reason I developed an interest in science, or your high school text, rather. Intro to Biology. That book taught me a basic truth.

KINSEY: And what truth would that be.

MR. X: That there's a logic behind everything. That it is possible to make sense of the world, and our place in it.

KINSEY: I'm flattered.

MR. X: I really am sorry about the nickname.

KINSEY: That's all right. I rather like it. You're welcome to use it. In private.

MR. X: Well. All right then. Prok it is. My friends call me Vic.

KINSEY: Really. I much prefer Victor. How is your dissertation coming.

MR. X: Well enough. I had Sarah look it over. She thinks I'm ready to present.

KINSEY: Very good. And you and Sarah. How are you two getting on?

            CLARA *is watching, listening.*

MR. X: We're both busy with our studies, but we manage to spend a few evenings a week together.

KINSEY: And what do you do? On your evenings together.

MR. X: We go for walks, or out for dinner. Sometimes we just stay in and study.

KINSEY: And your physical contact?

MR. X: My…

KINSEY: Your sexual contact.

MR. X: It's…well…limited…

KINSEY: Have you had intercourse yet?

MR. X: Of course not.

KINSEY: Have you discussed it?

MR. X: Well…no. I'm not quite sure how one would go about discussing it. It's not exactly dinner conversation.

KINSEY: It should be. Clara and I had trouble at first. A lot of that could have been avoided if we'd been able to

	communicate on that level. Of course, we also found out that part of the problem was her adherent clitoris.

MR. X: Adherent...

KINSEY: Yes. Thats why she wasn't receiving the proper amount of stimulation to render the act enjoyable. It was simply a matter of pulling back the veil of connective tissue over the clitoris and performing a blunt dissection. It was just a local. She didn't have to go under.

MR. X: Good God. You performed an operation on your wife's vagina?

KINSEY: Technically, the vagina and the clitoris are quite different, and of course I didn't perform the operation. It was done in a hospital, by a specialist.

MR. X: Of course. Of course it was.

KINSEY: Really Victor, use your common sense. I'm not a surgeon.

MR. X: Sorry.

KINSEY: My point is I would highly recommend starting the dialogue with Sarah as soon as possible. Do you masturbate?

MR. X: ...pardon?

KINSEY: Well, of course you do. Everyone does. Do you have a particular technique that you favour?

MR. X: No, not...really...

KINSEY: It's important that one becomes thoroughly familiar with the anatomy of the penis in order to maximize the amount of erotic irritation required to reach climax. Do you have books that you can refer to? I could lend you a few that I've found helpful. We could go over the material together. I'd be happy to field any questions, discuss techniques...

MR. X: I'm in love with Sarah. You know that, don't you?

KINSEY: Certainly. Would you like to borrow a book or two? I have one particularly comprehensive volume that covers both the male and female genitalia.

MR. X: I'd like that very much, Prok. Thank you.

KINSEY: You're welcome.

                  They fall into silence, KINSEY quite pleased with himself, MR. X studying him, unsure.

CLARA: *To the audience.* In University, my major was Chemistry. I used to believe that both the sexual and emotional response were chemically based, bits of molecular matter exchanged through touch, or floating on a breeze from one lover to another. I didn't believe in falling in love so much as finding the right molecules to combine with mine, to create something whole and larger. And then I fell in love with Prok, and I stopped being a scientist. I still believe that we can't help who we fall in love with, but the cause is something infinitely more complex than science.

                  KINSEY gets up and leaves MR. X, approaching CLARA.

KINSEY: Let me see your foot.

                  CLARA raises her foot. KINSEY removes her shoe, examines.

CLARA: What are you looking for.

KINSEY: I'm researching this marriage course they want me to teach. Came across a bit about foot fetishism in Havelock Ellis's Studies. How does this feel?

He sucks one of her toes.

CLARA: *Giggling.* It tickles.

KINSEY: Do you find it stimulating?

CLARA: Well... it's...

> *KINSEY continues to orally work CLARA's feet.*

...actually it's quite nice.

> *KINSEY pulls back, examining her feet, trying to appreciate their aesthetic.*

KINSEY: Interesting. According to Ellis, foot fetishism is exceedingly common among the Southern Chinese. He states that for a Chinese husband his wife's foot is more interesting than her face. That's why the women bind their feet, to make them smaller, more attractive.

CLARA: It is nice, but I don't think I'd go that far. What do you think of them?

KINSEY: I can't say that I've ever looked at them as sexual signals before, but if they function as erogenous zones, it would stand to reason that some portion of the opposite sex would be attracted to them.

CLARA: Apparently, in some cases, entire cultures.

KINSEY: It's not conclusive, though. It's the same problem I find with all of Ellis's work. There's no methodology backing it up. It's random.

CLARA: He's a well respected researcher. His work must have some validity.

KINSEY: At least he's better than the rest. Kraft-Ebing and Freud and the lot. Everything with them is 'pathological' and 'deviant'. It's all a disease that needs to be cured. You simply can't make those conclusions without an adequate sample size. If one were to do the field work and discover that indeed, foot fetishism is a predominant trait in our species, it could hardly be called pathological or deviant.

CLARA: I suppose not, but you can't go around asking people if they like to suck toes.

KINSEY: Why not?

CLARA: Because it's private. It's none of your business.

KINSEY: We're scientists. Everything is our business.

CLARA: It's not about science. It's about intimacy, and intimacy is...well, it's...oh for heaven's sake, it's just private. We're human beings, not gall wasps.

KINSEY: When we were first married we had considerable trouble. If information had been there, it would have saved us a lot of worry. Don't you think?

CLARA: You're missing the point, Prok...

KINSEY: Would it not have been easier for us if relevant information had been available?

CLARA: Yes, I suppose, / but...

KINSEY: / Then what is wrong with the scientific pursuit of that information?

CLARA: Fine. How about I get things rolling then. I'll phone my mother and ask her if she's fellated my father lately. I'm sure she'll understand it's all in the name of science. Honestly. I don't know why I ever bother challenging you on these things.

KINSEY begins to suck her toes again.

All you really want to hear is 'Yes, you're right'. I should know better by now...

KINSEY: *(With CLARA's toes in his mouth.)* I'm sorry.

CLARA: It wouldn't bother me if I at least got the sense that you were listening to—Good God that's nice.

KINSEY disengages, looks up at her, smiles.

Well. I don't know about the rest of the world, but we seemed to have muddled our way through without a manual.

KINSEY: I'd like to talk to you about something.

CLARA: And what would that be.

KINSEY: I think we should have a child. *(CLARA smiles.)* What?

CLARA: Too late.

KINSEY: What do you mean.

CLARA: We're already having one. I just found out this afternoon. I was going to tell you at dinner.

KINSEY: We're having a baby?

CLARA: No dear, I'm having a baby.

KINSEY: How are you feeling. Are you okay? Do you need anything?

CLARA: *(Extending her foot.)* Hmm… let me think…

KINSEY smiles, terribly pleased with himself. He goes to work on her toes with gusto.

MR. X, who has been watching the KINSEYs, begins to sing a slow, thoughtful rendition of "Hello My Baby."

MR. X: Hello my baby, hello my honey, hello my ragtime gal…

KINSEY disengages from CLARA, looking at MR. X. MR. X gets up, goes over to him, pulling him to his feet.

...Send me a kiss by wire, baby my heart's on fire,

If you refuse me, honey you'll lose me, then you'll be left alone...

MR. X and KINSEY begin a slow waltz, KINSEY joining in the singing, drifting into a dream, CLARA's imagining.

MR. X and
KINSEY: So baby, telephone and tell me I'm your own.

KINSEY gently rests his head on Mr. X's chest. The waltz ends. KINSEY slowly pulls away from MR. X. CLARA addresses the audience.

CLARA: Of course, in this life, all things joyful are tempered with heartbreak. It's a divine law, I think, designed to keep us whole, and humble.

Victor had gotten himself a job. Assistant Professor of Biology at Boston University. He moved away. Prok never talked about it. To look at him you'd think he didn't care one way or the other. But he kept a picture of Victor on the upper right hand corner of his desk, for the rest of his life. There were no pictures of us, his family. Only Victor.

Through the following, KINSEY kneels down and begins to pry open a floor board. CLARA watches.

I found the toothbrush just after Victor left. I was hugely pregnant, and cleaning the house from top to bottom for the third time that month, some maternal instinct driving me to sterilize every aspect of our lives, and I was cleaning out the attic, and I noticed this loose piece of planking, and I moved it and there it was.

KINSEY removes an old, worn, wooden toothbrush from beneath the loose floor board.

A single, worn, discolored toothbrush, all by itself.

KINSEY is examining the toothbrush, rolling it between his fingers. CLARA is watching him, silent, remembering...

Big band swing jazz music from the 1930s slams in. It plays throughout the following.

MR. X addresses the audience. His voice is amplified, larger than life.

MR. X: Dear Prok, Well well well. Congratulations are in order. Sara and I were overjoyed to hear that Clara is with child again. Number three. My goodness. Where have the years gone?

KINSEY puts away the toothbrush, collecting himself.

Throughout the following, CLARA retrieves and puts on her wedding dress and hiking boots.

Very sorry to hear about your oldest. One of my colleagues at the University, Dr. Hithers, has a child with thyrotoxicosis. He says the worst part is the bulging eyes—a constant reminder that something is wrong. Dr. Hithers sends his regards and invites you to write him if you'd like to open a dialogue concerning treatments.

KINSEY begins to study slides for his marriage course, taking notes.

Slide image: a black and white cross-section line drawing of male genitalia.

On a brighter note, Sara and I have some news of our own. It seems that we'll be joining you in the great adventure of parenthood, Prok. Yes, my friend, the pecker is in fine working order, and we'll soon have the progeny to prove it.

Slide image: a black and white cross-section line drawing of female genitalia.

Well, that's all for now, I think. Coming off a nasty bout of pneumonia that doesn't seem to want to go away. Other than that, all is well.

Slide image: a black and white cross-section line drawing of a penis entering a vagina.

KINSEY turns off the slide projector.

Look forward to your next letter, my friend. Say hello to Clara. All my best. Yours, Victor.

MR. X takes a seat, watching the Kinseys. CLARA has on the wedding dress and hiking boots. She's pregnant, and showing. She's dancing to the 30s big band swing jazz music, stomping and whirling, delirious.

KINSEY approaches, stops, watches her.

KINSEY: What in God's name are you doing?

CLARA, breathing heavily, stops, makes her way over to the record, lifts the needle. The music stops.

CLARA: My breasts have gotten bigger. Look at them. I'm busting out of this thing. The hiking boots still fit though. They feel a little bit heavier than I remember them, but they're still comfortable.

KINSEY: Where are the children?

CLARA: Napping.

KINSEY: How they could sleep through that awful racket is beyond me. Where did you get it.

CLARA: Victor sent it from Boston. There's a letter, too.

KINSEY: I can't believe he still holds out hope that I might be converted.

CLARA: Don't be such a snob.

CLARA begins to take off her hiking boots. KINSEY stands there, watching.

KINSEY: Are you feeling alright?

CLARA: I'm fine. By the way, the neighbors are complaining again. About you doing the gardening in your birthday suit.

KINSEY: That's ridiculous. I'm wearing a cover.

CLARA: It's not a cover. It's a loincloth. They think it's obscene, and I'm not entirely in disagreement with them.

KINSEY: What do you want me to do.

CLARA: It wouldn't make a lick of difference what I wanted you to do. I'm just passing on the message.

Silence.

KINSEY: How is Daniel today?

CLARA: He ate his lunch. He hasn't had any heart palpitations, or at least none that he's told me about. Did you know that he lies sometimes? To save me the worry. We had a weigh-in this morning. He's lost another two pounds. So. There it is. That's how Daniel is today.

KINSEY: I'll have a look at him when he gets up. We may have to adjust his diet.

CLARA: He told me about your little chat, Alfred. I won't have it.

KINSEY: What are you talking about.

CLARA: You know perfectly well what I'm talking about. You were asking him questions about his body. You asked him if he ever touched himself. You were interviewing him. You were taking his history, for God's sake.

KINSEY: He's a valid subject. We need to gain an understanding of pre-pubescent sexuality / in order to…

CLARA: / He is not a subject! He is your son. I will not have you encouraging sexual awareness in a three year old. It's not healthy. / It's not right.

KINSEY: / Give me a little credit. I am fully aware that he is my son. I would never do anything to harm him. I am simply collecting information as it already exists in his consciousness. I am not affecting that consciousness in any way whatsoever. I'd even suggest that it may be of / some benefit…

CLARA: / Listen to me. It will not be tolerated. I do not want him to become one of your statistics, and I do not need to justify that to you. I am simply forbidding it.

I need you to be a father. Just be his dad. Please.

KINSEY: We haven't exhausted the radiation therapy, Mac. Something may still come of that. And surgery is still an option. The success rate for thyroid gland reduction is encouragingly high. There's no need to worry yourself so.

CLARA: You aren't here with him all day long! I don't even recognize him anymore with those bulging, staring eyes, he looks like a frightened little animal, and there is nothing I can do except worry!

KINSEY: I'm just trying to help.

CLARA: Then let me know that I am not alone here. Let me know that you're worried too. Let me know that you're terrified of losing him, that you want to scream at God for letting this happen to your son. You let me see that, and then you can tell me that there's no need to worry myself so.

Silence.

KINSEY: Can I get you anything?

CLARA: No.

KINSEY: I'm going to go work in the garden. Send the children out when they get up. We can spend some time together before dinner.

            KINSEY heads for the garden. CLARA watches after him.

            The sound of birds and insects.

            KINSEY begins working. He is transplanting great mounds of flowers, moving sections of earth and plants.

            CLARA moves out to the garden area, watching KINSEY work.

KINSEY: *(To CLARA.)* Did you know that in Victorian England, flowers used to be a form of communication? Entire messages were sent with a bouquet. Lily of the Valley was the return of happiness, and the Goldenrod advised precaution. Periwinkle, a lovely bit of ground cover, was sweet remembrances. And the Iris, it held its own place in the language of flowers. The Iris signified that the whole was a message. It was the first thing the Victorian lover would look for. Without the telltale Iris, it was only a bouquet of flowers.

CLARA: There were no Marigolds in your garden, were there Prok.

            Silence.

KINSEY: My father used to plant them everywhere. In the language of flowers, the Marigold represents mental anguish, vulgar minds, jealousy, grief. In French, *souci* means worry. It also means

Marigold. The Caltha Palustri, a marsh Marigold, is able to grow in solid clay. I've always thought there is a certain darkness of soul in a plant that can grow in solid clay.

KINSEY stops working. Silence.

I was never taught how to be a good father. But I do try my best. I love our children, very much.

CLARA: I know.

KINSEY returns to his work. CLARA watches him.

MR. X has taken up a letter, and is reviewing it.

MR. X: Kinsey, can I see you for a moment?

KINSEY: Hmm? Yes, yes of course.

KINSEY brushes off the garden dirt and makes his way over to MR. X. CLARA goes back to her rocker.

What can I do for you, Dr. Wolfe?

MR. X: The better question might be what can I do for you. You've taken on quite the load this semester. How is the marriage course going?

KINSEY: I trust you've seen the enrollment figures.

MR. X: It's become one of the most popular courses on campus.

KINSEY: It's long overdue.

MR. X: And the research? How is that going?

KINSEY: How do you mean?

MR. X: The histories you're collecting. I was just wondering if you've had any resistance, any problems.

KINSEY: No.

MR. X: I see. Alfred, you know how strongly I support the work you're doing.

KINSEY: Certainly. You've been a great help to me.

MR. X: I think what you're doing is important. But as President of this University, I have to answer to a Board of Directors, and the community at large. There have been complaints.

KINSEY: From who?

MR. X: It seems the opposition is being focused by Father Smit, and I'm beginning to believe he may be just the tip of the iceberg.

KINSEY: Oh come on, Arnold. Smit is a puritan dinosaur. He speaks with an echo that goes back to the eighteen hundreds. Surely you don't take seriously any criticism he may level.

MR. X: Father Smit heads the largest church in Bloomington. His voice carries considerable weight. And he's not alone. Professor Sheffman has filed a formal complaint against you, and it seems a committee of physicians is forming in protest / on the grounds that...

KINSEY: / What's Sheffman's problem.

MR. X: Well, to begin with, I don't think you helped matters by throwing her out of your class and disclaiming her lecture.

KINSEY: I invited her into my class as a guest lecturer with the caveat that she rigorously follow my course outline. She failed to do that. I asked her to leave.

MR. X: You publicly embarrassed her. You know Sheffman. She's not going to let that slide. She's answering you by filing a formal complaint concerning your private meetings with the students. She's accusing you of using the course for research instead of education.

KINSEY: The course is a perfect vehicle for both, both of which are fundamentally needed. Of course the two are going to be entwined. It's only practical.

MR. X: We knew we'd get resistance on this, Al. We have to be sensitive to the larger community, and that, at times, is going to mean that you are not always going to get your way. It's the business of education. And for your work to continue, I have to keep that business healthy.

KINSEY: So what do you want me to do?

MR. X: I want you to discontinue your interviews with the students.

KINSEY: But that's the backbone of my research! It's the core of my sample size. For this work to have any validity, I need an adequate sample size. You're / asking me to...

MR. X: / Al, that is enough! I am not the enemy. You can continue collecting histories, with my blessing, but I'm asking you to confine your activities to the faculty and to whoever else you may solicit outside of the University. I could care less who you talk to off campus, go ask Father Smit if he's buggered any of the nuns for all I care, just stay away from the students!

KINSEY: And what of the students that seek me out for advice and counselling. Shall I turn them away? Is that what you're asking me to do?

MR. X: Of course not. That is a private matter between you and them. I am asking you, however, to refrain from taking their histories.

KINSEY: Fine.

MR. X: Thank you.

KINSEY: And if I discover that Father Smit is buggering the
                nuns, I will make an exception to my rule of
                confidentiality. I promise you'll be the first to
                know.

MR. X: I suppose this would be the time for a bit of good
                news.

KINSEY: And what good news would that be.

MR. X: Just a little note from the Rockefeller Foundation
                informing us that we've been awarded our grant to
                formalize your research.

                We got our grant, Prok.

KINSEY: Brilliant, brilliant work, my friend! Well done. I
                knew we'd get it.

MR. X: It's not a huge amount of money, and it's not
                directly from the Rockefeller. They filtered it
                through a sub-committee, but if we can produce
                some initial results, we can go after operating
                money next year. It'll go a long way to legitimize
                the work you're doing.

KINSEY: I should say so. The first thing we should do is
                spread the word. Let Sheffman and Smit chew on
                this for a while. That should put a plug in things.

MR. X: The Rockefeller is touchy on this, that's why
                they're keeping us at a distance. If we start
                gloating, all we've accomplished is to give Smit
                and his cronies a year to lobby against us. We
                proceed quietly. No fuss. No bother. Alright?

KINSEY: I can do that.

MR. X: And no student interviews.

KINSEY: No student interviews. Scout's honour.

MR. X: Thank you. Congratulations, Professor Kinsey.

KINSEY: Thank you, Doctor Wolfe.

                  They shake hands.

                  Big band swing music.

                  CLARA has been reading from a document, retrieved from the storage crate beside her rocker.

                  KINSEY approaches, watches her. Music fades under.

CLARA: *(Noticing KINSEY.)* Why are you home so early?

KINSEY: I'm having problems with my trainees. With the interview. I need to discuss it with you.

                  Silence. KINSEY stands there, waiting.

CLARA: Go ahead.

KINSEY: I need them to maintain a direct tone without intimidating the subject. I'm having difficulty teaching them the right balance.

CLARA: Why is it necessary to 'maintain a direct tone'.

KINSEY: Because of the private nature of the subject matter. It's imperative that the questions be without hesitation and without apology. If the interviewer shows embarrassment, what can one possibly expect from the subject.

CLARA: And this has never come up before?

KINSEY: I've never had people working for me before. I've always done all the interviewing myself. I've never had to articulate how it's done.

                  CLARA puts the document back in the crate, looks at KINSEY, taking him in, smiling.

CLARA: Come here. Sit down.

KINSEY does.

Interview me. Collect my history.

KINSEY: You've already given me your history.

CLARA: Not all of it.

Silence.

KINSEY: Really.

CLARA: Prok, a stranger is not going to trust you with personal information unless you establish a connection first. A camaraderie. A direct tone is important, absolutely, but it can also be very intimidating, don't you think?

KINSEY: Have I not been satisfying you?

CLARA: What are you talking about?

KINSEY: Sexually. Have I not been satisfying you.

CLARA: We're talking about the interview.

KINSEY: I'm aware of that. I'm also newly aware there are things you feel you can't tell me.

CLARA: *(Smiling.)* You're angry with me.

KINSEY: No.

CLARA: Yes you are.

KINSEY: No I'm not. But I do very much want to know what you feel you can't trust me with.

CLARA: So find out. Interview me.

Silence.

KINSEY: When did you first tire of your marriage?

CLARA: Oh for heaven's sake, Prok. Don't be silly.

KINSEY: Shall I repeat the question?

CLARA: If you can't retain your objectivity, there's no point in doing this.

KINSEY: When did you first tire of your marriage?

CLARA :   I'm not tired of it.

KINSEY: How often have you thought of leaving your husband?

CLARA: Honestly, Al, this really is / silly.

KINSEY: / How often have you / thought...

CLARA: / Never. I have never thought of leaving you.

KINSEY: How many affairs have you had in the course of your marriage?

CLARA: None.

KINSEY: How many times have you thought of having an affair?

CLARA: *(She hesitates.)* Never.

KINSEY: Would you say that you are satisfied with your love life.

CLARA: Yes.

KINSEY: What are the sexual activities you would like to engage in that you aren't presently engaged in?

CLARA: There aren't any.

KINSEY: When you fantasize about other men, is your husband present?

            Silence.

CLARA: You focus the question on the husband, and assume the fantasies. Therefore the subject assumes that you already know, and that you aren't passing judgement. Very clever.

KINSEY goes to her, cuddles her.

KINSEY: Is that your big secret? That you fantasize about other men?

CLARA: One of them.

KINSEY pulls back, looks at CLARA, smiles and then gives her a kiss, sweet and chaste, as if he were kissing a child.

Sound of insects, distorted and brushed with something deeper and distant, possibly sex, or discomfort.

KINSEY leaves CLARA, taking his place at his desk, and begins working. He stops, picks up the picture of Victor from the corner of his desk, looks at it. CLARA watches him.

The soundscape fades. MR. X approaches KINSEY.

MR. X: Dr. Kinsey?

KINSEY returns Victor's picture, pretends busyness.

KINSEY: David, yes.

MR. X: Am I interrupting?

KINSEY: No, no, that's fine.

MR. X: What are you working on?

KINSEY: Just quantifying some histories. Endless work, but it will eventually be the backbone of my research. It has to be done. What can I do for you?

MR. X: I'd like to apply for one of the assistant positions.

KINSEY: Oh. I see.

MR. X:	I'm assuming you're still taking applications. The posting indicated the deadline is next week.
KINSEY:	You did well in my taxonomy course. 87 percent, if I'm not mistaken.
MR. X:	I think that's right. How did you remember that? That was three years ago.
KINSEY:	I don't give out many A's. I'm leaning heavily on the basic principles of species classification to establish groupings for quantifying the data. I must warn you, the work can be quite tedious, and the rewards are few and far between. It takes a particular constitution to tolerate the long hours.
MR. X:	It's amazing what one can tolerate when one is sufficiently interested in the subject matter.

Silence.

KINSEY:	Yes. Of course. David, would you be interested in contributing your history?
MR. X:	Sure, if you'd like.
KINSEY:	I'd like that very much. Have a seat. Make yourself comfortable.
MR. X:	Thanks.
KINSEY:	Why don't you tell me a little about yourself. What you do for entertainment, what kind of music you like, that sort of thing.
MR. X:	Well, let's see, I'm partial to jazz, mostly…
KINSEY:	Good for you. That's all I listen to. And what do you do with your weekends, David.

Sound of big band swing music builds in.

MR. X:	I enjoy a bit of theatre, but mostly the movies, and I like the dance clubs, you know, the big band clubs, that sort of thing.

KINSEY listens attentively, smiling and nodding, surreptitiously taking notes, as the big band swing music drowns out MR. X.

Soundscape fades under. CLARA, in her rocker, addresses the audience.

CLARA: When Prok started his research, human beings were thought to be naturally monogamous.

MR. X gets up and positions himself between KINSEY's legs, undoing his pants.

So were South American Tamarin monkeys. It was eventually scientifically confirmed that although the monkeys do form marriage bonds, infidelity rates were as high as a third of all pairs in a given year.

MR. X continues to crouch between KINSEY's legs. It is unclear what he is doing.

Which, it turns out, corresponds almost exactly to the rate of infidelity in human marriages which, in turn, suggests that it's a natural phenomenon in our species as well.

I'm sure that makes a third of you feel a lot better.

CLARA returns her attention to MR. X and KINSEY.

MR. X gets up, picks up a clipboard, makes a note. KINSEY does up his trousers through the following.

MR. X: It's a nasty infection, there's no doubt about that.

KINSEY: I'm assuming it's treatable.

MR. X: I'll write you a prescription for some antibiotics, and a period of inactivity will be necessary. Have a seat.

KINSEY: I'd self-diagnosed as much. I almost didn't bother you with it, Dr. Medley, but seeing as how we already had an appointment about Daniel, I thought better safe than sorry. I assume his test results are in?

MR. X writes KINSEY a prescription through the following.

MR. X: Yes. It's quite interesting actually, and ultimately I believe it's good news. He's still manufacturing excessive thyroxin, we'll have to step up the iodine treatments, and increase the level of radioactivity. If we can't achieve suppression then I don't see any other option but to remove part of the gland.

KINSEY: Your idea of good news and mine differ considerably.

MR. X: Well, this is where it gets complicated. We think now that Daniel may be diabetic, and we think that a huge part of the tissue damage that we were attributing to the hyperthyroid condition may not even be related to it.

KINSEY: Diabetic?

MR. X: Yes.

KINSEY: How could I have missed that.

MR. X: The symptoms are very similar. The important thing is that we know now, and we can treat the diabetes separately.

KINSEY: Yes. Yes, of course. Another round of tests will be in order. We'll need to isolate the pancreas for damage, and get some proper insulin readings.

MR. X: He's going to be alright, Al.

KINSEY: Of course he is. I'll have to confer with Clara, but I'm sure we'll want to have him back here as soon as possible. *Preparing to leave.* Thank you for your time. It's appreciated.

MR. X: Al, just a quick word, if you will. It's fairly obvious from the nature of your infection that there has been intrusion, I would think massive intrusion, by some form of foreign object. Your urethra is showing considerable distress. I suspect the split in the opening is irreparable.

           Silence.

KINSEY: Yes?

MR. X: As a physician I'm advising you that whatever behavior is causing the damage needs to cease immediately. From a health standpoint, it's imperative.

KINSEY: I understand. Thank you. Good day, Dr. Medley.

MR. X: Dr. Kinsey.

           KINSEY leaves the area and approaches CLARA, who's been watching. She is in her rocker, waiting for KINSEY, who calls into the house.

KINSEY: Mac, I'm home!

CLARA: I'm in the drawing room.

           KINSEY approaches.

           Come, sit. I need to talk to you.

KINSEY: What is it.

CLARA: Sarah called last night, from Boston. It seems Victor has been hospitalized with tuberculosis. He's been having respiratory problems for some time, more so than he's been letting on. It's bad, Prok. I was thinking that perhaps we could drive up and see them after we're finished with Daniel's tests.

KINSEY: I don't know that I…I don't know that I can take the time off right now.

CLARA: It would only be a few extra days.

KINSEY: I need to have my assistants in place by the end of the semester, and I don't know of anyone who could take over my lectures.

CLARA: Al… it's Victor. Your work can wait.

KINSEY: I'll…I'll make the arrangements…for a summer trip. Daniel should be somewhat better by then, we can take the children and make it a holiday. It surely can't be that bad. I just spoke with him a month ago. He was fine.

CLARA: Sarah didn't sound very positive. If nothing else, she could certainly use a little support right now.

KINSEY: I'll see what I can do.

CLARA: Prok…I'm sorry. I know how much he means to you.

KINSEY: Yes. Well. Thank you.

            KINSEY takes his lecture position. MR. X joins him as David, now his teaching assistant, sitting off to one side, working the slide projector.

            Slide image: A black and white photo of engorged female genitalia.

            And here we have an example of the female genitalia in full arousal. Note the blood engorged labia major, and the swollen clitoris. You can also see the labia minor parting to accommodate the insertion of the penis.

            Slide image: A black and white photo of an erect penis.

            The stimulated male genitalia responds in much

the same way, engorging itself with blood to increase sensitivity and to stiffen in order to facilitate penetration. The size of both the male and female genitalia varies considerably, more so…more so with the male than female. However, except in cases of extreme variation, the size does not *(KINSEY is having trouble focusing.)* …it…the size…does not adversely affect function, either in terms of…of…

MR. X: Dr. Kinsey?

KINSEY: Yes Victor.

MR. X: It's…it's David, Dr. Kinsey.

> *CLARA, in her rocker, watches KINSEY.*

KINSEY: What?

MR. X: You called me Victor.

KINSEY: Did I? I'm sorry. David. You…you had an observation.

MR. X: Yes, I was thinking you might want to point out to the class the similarities between the clitoris and the penis in terms of their biological function, in terms of both being the centre of the sexual response.

KINSEY: Yes, well, certainly the two are vastly different organs, both in terms of their physiology and their function, but they are undeniably…they are undeniably…

> *KINSEY bows his head and begins to cry.*

MR. X: Professor Kinsey? Are you all right?

KINSEY: I seem to be a bit distracted at the moment. Perhaps it would be best if we cut the lecture short. I'll pick up here tomorrow. Thank you.

KINSEY makes his way into his garden. Throughout the following, he disrobes, stripping down to his loincloth. He begins to tear up his garden, his plants and flowers, moving great mounds of earth from one location to the other. The sound of insects brushes in, a distant hum.

CLARA addresses the audience.

CLARA: Our son Daniel died. And then Victor died.

I know how betrayed Prok felt, how useless all his knowledge was in the face of these simple biological breakdowns. A son's gland that doesn't work properly, or a germ that manages to find its way into the lungs of a friend. Such simple things, really, and yet completely beyond his control. His science had failed him. But nothing changed, to look at the man. He just fixed his spine a little straighter, got a little more stubborn, a little more driven.

Sometimes we aren't able to bury our dead. Something happens, an event, or a circumstance, and Time intervenes and takes over and bullies us on, and we're forced to carry our dead with us. There is no resolution. Only a soul that weighs on us infinitely more in death than it did in life.

KINSEY is working himself into a frenzy in the garden, ripping and gouging, trying to create something perfect. CLARA and MR. X watch him. The sound of insects builds.

When I look back on those times, before The Book, I think we may have all been asleep. All those years, through the depression, and the war…not as individuals, certainly not, but collectively, as a culture, there was a part of us, an awareness, that was asleep, dormant, just under the surface, waiting…waiting for Prok…

KINSEY is now a fury in the garden.

We wouldn't have to wait long.

The lights fade, as the sound of insects distorts and deepens and builds to a din, a plague.

End of Act I.

ACT II

The Knowledge of Good and Evil

Light finds MR. X, dressed in a beret and sunglasses. Percussion builds in, slow and smokey. He is enjoying himself, playing the cool beatnik. He's good at it.

BEAT POET: Before Betty Furness became the queen of appliances and McCarthy was starting his hunt for communist alliances there was no McDonald's although it wasn't far away frozen TV Dinners were the meal of the day before *Playboy* before James Dean kids still used words like neato and keen jazz set the beat for Kerouac in heat diddlin' Cassady and dating mary jane travelling their way to fortune and fame.

On the road.

And all the blacks sat at the back of the bus and they weren't allowed to put up a fuss and Ozzie and Harriet were still a concept then and the Beav hadn't been born yet when Milton Berle was the King of TV and they called it the land of the brave and the free.

And everyone smoked.

No one had sex that's what they all said and when they did have sex it was proper in bed with the lights off they did it lying head to head and only for babies and only when wed and then along comes Kinsey with a stat or two apparently everyone had sex apparently nothing was new men slept with men and women with women married people cheated and then were forgiven animals too arrived on the scene and the kids were all doing it in their mid-teens and the question I have what doesn't make sense if they're all having sex why's everyone tense all the fuss and the bother the beating of breasts the oh my's the good gods the denial fest good bloody Christ what a stink Kinsey made with the truth of how often we were all getting laid.

Dig it.

Percussion ends.

Lights find CLARA, in full gardening regalia. She takes in MR. X.

CLARA: Show off.

MR. X takes off his beatnik gear, and settles in to watch and listen. CLARA takes in the garden, assessing her task. She addresses the audience.

What a mess.

In the language of flowers I think this is called verbiage diarrhoea. I'm just going after this one little corner. The hell with the rest of it. I want to grow some tomatoes. I don't know if tomatoes mean anything, if there's a language of fruits and vegetables, but to me, they mean heaven. A fresh tomato sandwich, toasted, with just a bit of butter, and salt and pepper. Nothing else. You've arrived at the pearly gates.

She looks over the garden again, remembering.

Prok started to let the garden go after Daniel and Victor passed on. He just walked away from it. There was nothing I could do. I had my hands full raising four kids.

Three. Three kids.

Well, four if you counted Prok.

She digs into the weeds, getting down to business.

The first volume came out in the summer of 1948. *Sexual Behavior in the Human Male.* Prok and I called it The Book. As if it were the only one in the world. Everybody wanted a piece of him after The Book came out. I used to tell my friends that I hardly saw him at night anymore since he took up sex. He was either holed up at the Institute, or lecturing, or collecting histories, or giving speeches, or meeting the press. He was a star. He knew it, too. Played it like he was born to it. He played it like only a true star can—as if he wasn't a star at all, as if being on a dozen magazine covers was the most natural thing in the world. And the storm just got bigger and bigger, until, if you were to believe the papers and the radio and the film reels and the magazines, Prok's fat old boring book was going to change the world. Or already had.

I stayed home through most of it. The kids were all grown up by then, so I helped out at the Institute a bit, but I kept a pretty low profile. I smiled and nodded and said the right things and let them take a few pictures and they pretty much left me alone. It was Prok they wanted. I was just a prop.

Throughout the following, light slowly finds KINSEY, shaking hands, signing autographs, smiling politely, nodding, a dream that CLARA can see.

And then for no particular reason I decided to go with him on one of his road trips. He was giving a speech at a convention in New York and, quite frankly, I was bored with the Institute, and bored with my empty home, so I went with him. To New York City.

Well. I couldn't believe the fuss. Everywhere we went, there were flashbulbs, and reporters, and people asking for his autograph. His autograph. It was surreal. He was still the same man I knew, he was still Prok, but standing there, a famous person, at the centre of all that fuss and bother, standing there as if it was the way things should be, as if all that attention should be his...it was like looking at the negative instead of the picture.

KINSEY fades.

I couldn't have possibly gotten away from it all fast enough. So, I left him at the convention, droning on about sexual variations to a bunch of crusty old scientists, and me and the other wives, we all ended up at a Broadway musical. *Kiss Me Kate.*

"It's Too Darn Hot," from Kiss Me Kate, *builds under her monologue.*

"It's too darn hot, it's too darn hot, I'd like to sup with my baby tonight, and play the pup with my baby tonight, but I ain't up to my baby tonight, cause it's too darn hot..."

And before the curtain went up, just as everyone was settling, they dimmed the lights and someone came out with a microphone, to this day I still don't know who that person was, but he came out and welcomed me to the performance. "Ladies and Gentlemen, we have a celebrity with us this evening. Mrs. Alfred C. Kinsey. Tonight's show is in your honour, Mrs. Kinsey" and a spotlight swung around and pinned me to my seat, like a bug on a corkboard, and everyone applauded and I was utterly, completely horrified.

"It's too darn hot, it's too darn hot, I'd like to sup with my baby tonight, and play the pup with my baby tonight, but I ain't up to my baby tonight, cause it's too darn hot...

Why were they doing that? How did they even know I was there? I don't think, to this day, I have ever felt so completely uncomfortable, and then the show started and I'm sure I missed the entire first act.

> *"According to the Kinsey Report, every average man you know, much prefers to play his favourite sport when the temperature is low, but when the thermometer goes way up and the weather is sizzling hot, mister Adam for his madam is not."*

And then right at the beginning of the second act, The Book is mentioned in one of the songs, and I thought ah, that's what this is all about, and I started to actually pay attention to the play, and I realized it was a show about people in show business.

> *"It's too darn hot, it's too darn hot, I'd like to sup with my baby tonight, and play the pup with my baby tonight, but I ain't up to my baby tonight, cause it's too darn hot."*

It was a musical within a musical, and I became acutely aware that I was living my own version of that. A show within a show. It was what my husband's life had become, and what mine was threatening to become, simply through association.

> *The musical score fades to silence.*

For the rest of my life I would call them "Kiss Me Kate" moments, those moments when I could see clearly that irony, that contradiction, the two worlds, co-existing, one within the other. Prok and I, alone, just the two of us, and Prok and I at the centre of this impossibly complex web, this whole other world that had nothing to do with us, really, but only existed because of us, because of him. A show within a show.

A "Kiss Me Kate" moment...

CLARA takes in the ravaged garden.

Now there's just me. Me at the centre of a big bunch of weeds.

That's okay. I know better than to bite off more than I can chew. Just this one little corner. That's all I want. A little batch of tomatoes.

Slide image: A black and white picture of two men having anal intercourse, missionary position.

CLARA ploughs into the weeds with gusto, ripping and gouging great handfuls, a dervish. She weeds in much the same way as KINSEY planted at the end of Act I. She continues reclaiming throughout KINSEY's lecture.

Light finds KINSEY, who is taking his place for his lecture.

Slide image: A black and white picture of two men having anal intercourse, doggy style.

KINSEY: This illustrates the most common position, but as you've seen, it is by no means the only one. There are as many variations as one could imagine, most of them being similar to coital positions. And of course anal intercourse is certainly not exclusive to homosexual couplings. You will find statistical evidence of this on page 579 of *Sexual Behavior in the Human Male*. In fact, in sixteen years of study, I have yet to find any sexual act that is unique to any one person or one situation. One might say, to use a musical metaphor, that there are only so many notes that can be played. There may be an infinite number of combinations, but there are only so many notes. In that context, a physiological context, everything must be considered normal. Everything is normal, or nothing is. There is no gray area.

CLARA plunks down in the garden, exhausted, resting.

KINSEY takes a seat, pulls out a clipboard and pen. MR. X joins him, sitting opposite. Throughout the following, X studies KINSEY intently. KINSEY is calm, waiting patiently, returning his gaze. It is a subtle test of wills.

CLARA: Prok wasn't the first, by the way, to talk about sex. Some thirty years before him, in 1918, there was a sex manual written by a woman. *Married Love*, by Dr. Marie Stopes. It was an excellent, straightforward guide, largely ignored because it was written by a woman, and in 1918 women were not considered sexual beings. They were considered receptacles for penises.

Prok knew about her work. He thought the manual was quite good. He never addressed it in public though. He was afraid people wouldn't take him seriously.

CLARA picks herself up, cleans herself off. Throughout the following, she gets out of her gardening regalia, and puts her tools away.

KINSEY: Would you like to do this another day, my friend?

MR. X: Why do you call me that? "My friend."

KINSEY: What would you like me to call you?

MR. X: Did you know the word 'friend' comes from the proto Germanic *frijojanan* meaning free, and *frijon* meaning love? Free love. Friend.

KINSEY: It actually predates that, back through the Old English to a Greek root.

MR. X: You know Greek?

KINSEY: It's one of the languages of science. What would you like me to call you?

MR. X: Call me by my name.

KINSEY: Very well, Mr. Lawrence. Would you like to continue with your history, or shall we pick it up another day?

MR. X: Do you remember when we met?

KINSEY: Yes, of course.

> CLARA *returns to her rocker, begins sorting through a crate she's packing for storage.*

MR. X: I'd heard of you, before we met. Well, everyone had heard of you. It was at a party in New York, a literary thing, wasn't it?

KINSEY: Yes.

MR. X: It was a particularly 'gay' evening if I recall—all the biggies were there—Gore Vidal, Ginsberg, Burroughs, and somebody was in the washroom getting a blowjob, I think it was Wheeler, and everyone was stoned and drunk and half-naked and into the middle of all that walks the infamous Alfred C. Kinsey. Bam. The world stops.

KINSEY: I don't think I had as much impact as you're giving me credit for, Mr. Lawrence.

MR. X: Don't kid yourself, 'my friend.' That little party you'd walked into, that little group of people, they were the edge, they were beyond cool. You had to be something pretty special to impress those people. And when you walked in? Every one of them, absolutely everybody, practically impaled themselves trying to get your attention. You could have had any one of them that night.

> CLARA *has found a document in the crate that obviously interests her. She begins to read through it.*

KINSEY: Perhaps we should pick this up another day.

MR. X: Am I embarrassing you? Isn't that interesting. You shouldn't be shy about it. It's who you are. You carry the torch. You're at the front of the pack, taking everything that they do in private, all the things that they're still ashamed of, you take it all and you walk into the centre of the world and hold it up and say Look. Look at this. It exists, and it's normal, and there's nothing to be ashamed of. You're the only one doing that, and you're being heard all the way round the world, announcing that we're all normal, we're okay. That's why you could have had any one of them that night. You're their hero.

KINSEY: You said "we," Mr. Lawrence.

MR. X: What?

KINSEY: You said "announcing that we're all normal, we're okay," and then you switched back to "them." Why?

MR. X: I say "we" instead of "them" so now I'm a queer boy. Right? I'm subconsciously associating. Don't insult me, Doc. I'm a little more complicated than that.

KINSEY: I thought you might be associating yourself with them because you perceive them as important people, Mr. Lawrence. I've collected enough of your history to know your sexual expression is not catagorical.

                 Silence.

                 Would you like to continue?

MR. X: I think that'll be enough for today.

                 CLARA stops reading and puts the document back in the crate.

KINSEY: I'll look forward to our next interview.

                 KINSEY gathers himself and leaves. MR. X picks up KINSEY's clipboard, begins taking notes.

                 CLARA addresses the audience.

CLARA: Did you know the word "Bible" comes from the Greek *Byblos*, meaning...The Book. When I discovered this, I brought it to Prok's attention because we'd been referring to his book as The Book. I thought it was funny. He called it an "unfortunate coincidence."

                 It got me thinking, though. About sex, and the Bible. Taken literally, everything after the apple was a mistake. We were never supposed to have the knowledge of Good and Evil. It wasn't part of the plan. Ipso facto, everything that followed was not supposed to happen. We've been in one huge chaotic free fall since the beginning of time, and it all started with a little piece of fruit and some nooky.

                 Of course, that was all a woman's fault. Poor old Eve...

                 She gets up and retrieves a tray full of dirty glasses, ashtrays, an almost empty bottle of Scotch.

                 I wonder if they had good sex. Adam and Eve. I hope so. Otherwise, what was the point.

MR. X: Where's Prok?

                 CLARA approaches MR. X with the tray.

CLARA: He's driving people home. I didn't know you were still here, David. Everyone else has left already. Did you get everything you needed?

MR. X: The film ran out early, but we got most of it.

CLARA: That was a lively group. I thought that one girl was going to hurt herself. I didn't know a back could bend that way. Would you like a drink? There's some Scotch left...

MR. X: No, thanks. I still have notes to do. It was a pretty hands-on night. I didn't have much of a chance to get anything else done.

CLARA: I always find it quite interesting when you dive into the proceedings. You seem to enjoy your work.

MR. X: Sometimes it's necessary, to get things started, or to show people what we need. We're after specific activities, things we haven't recorded yet, variations. It's easier to set up when you're in it.

CLARA: Of course. All in the name of science.

MR. X: Are you alright?

CLARA: I'm just a little tired. I don't seem to have the objectivity you and the others do. You're all so removed from it, taking your notes and filing it all away, just another day's work.

MR. X: It's my job. I'm a scientist. Everything is normal, or nothing is.

CLARA: Do you really believe that?

Silence.

Can I talk to you about Prok?

MR. X: Sure.

CLARA: He was having trouble sleeping, and he started taking something for it. I don't know what exactly, he hides it from me, he thinks I don't know. I suspect it's some sort of barbituate. And I think he may be taking amphetamines as well, to bring himself back in the morning. He's not sleeping at all anymore, David. He seems to be horribly distracted at times, and I'm noticing physical deterioration.

MR. X: I see it too. The distance, and the fatigue. Have you tried to talk to him about it?

CLARA: Of course. But it's Prok. There's no point in talking. I don't know what to do.

MR. X: I don't know if there's anything you can do, Clara, except be there for him.

Silence.

You know you're a help to all of us, here. Your presence, what you do for us, it makes the Institute...well, you make it feel like home.

CLARA: Lemonade and apple pie is home, David. Cocktails and dainties at a Wednesday night orgy is just strange.

MR. X: It doesn't feel strange. Not when you're doing it.

Silence.

CLARA: Are you sure you wouldn't like a drink?

MR. X: Maybe one.

CLARA pours them drinks.

KINSEY at his podium, lecturing to the audience. He is tired, but still absolutely lucid and in control.

KINSEY: Our objective understanding of the world around us is in conflict with our subjective response to it. We know what is right, what is morally and ethically good, what is expected of us by the society in which we live. But what is expected of us is so often in conflict with what we feel, what we want. This is the dilemma of the human condition. The perplexity that accompanies reason. And with reason comes consciousness, and with consciousness comes a conscience, and with a conscience comes shame. And who among us does not know shame? Who among us can stand up and say that they have led a life that is morally and ethically pure, in thought and deed? A life lived as an open book. A life lived shamelessly.

CLARA and MR. X begin to touch each other, gently.

But. If we do something that causes us shame only in the eyes of others, so we choose to keep what we do a secret, is it then a shameless action? Because no one knows about it, does that make the behavior beyond moral and ethical judgement? And in whose eyes are we judging the behavior? Who decides what is morally and ethically reprehensible? The Church? The State? Under whose authority?

MR. X begins to make love to CLARA. It is slow, and sensuous. He is gorgeously gentle with her. They look beautiful together.

A theory. A hypothesis, if you will. What if. What if the arbiter of all that is morally and ethically good isn't an objective entity? What if the arbiter isn't a set of rules, isn't a code of behavior, or a list of rights and wrongs? What if we're making it up? What if there is no God, or Gods, or anything higher or more omnipotent? What if we aren't answering to anybody, or anything, except ourselves? What if we're just animals, and the only guiding principle we have is survival? Survival of the species, and survival of the fittest within that species. If this were the case, then we would all be free to do whatever we wanted to do, shamelessly, and the repercussions for our actions would come at the hands of other individuals doing what they wanted to do. And if the fittest of those individuals ended up being murderers and pedophiles and rapists and thieves, then so be it. That would be the natural order of things.

But I don't believe that would be the outcome. I believe that if the only arbiter of what is right and what is wrong came from within, our subjective response to the world around us, if the societal blanket of moral and ethical tyranny was lifted and we were released to be ourselves, to answer only to ourselves, I believe our species would transcend anything that we have ever imagined, that our innate goodness and love and understanding and compassion would rise up and make the murderers and pedophiles and rapists and thieves gasp and ache with a recognition of something they could never have. I believe that we would become the God that we seek.

MR. X slowly pulls away from CLARA.

That is what I believe.

The sound of insects brushes in, faint and distant.

MR. X: She was a saucy little thing, it was all come here, go away, but she enjoyed it. They all enjoy it, if you're nice. This one did.

             KINSEY joins him, surreptitiously taking notes throughout the following. CLARA returns to her rocker, watching the two of them.

KINSEY: Where did you meet her, Mr. Lawrence?

MR. X: At the soda shop on Davies.

KINSEY: Did you buy her a soda?

MR. X: She didn't need it. She was ready when she walked in.

KINSEY: How old do you think she was?

MR. X: Eleven, maybe twelve. Her hips were just starting to go.

          The sound of insects begins to grow louder.

KINSEY: What attracted you to her?

MR. X: I'm in charge here. I'll tell you what you need to know.

          CLARA, who is still watching, listening, seems drained by the exchange.

KINSEY: Yes, of course. Take your time, Mr. Lawrence.

MR. X: I'll tell you about the walk home. We went through the park, so she could look at all the lilac bushes. She liked the smell. That's when she started to get difficult. She started to get sassy with me, all come here go away come here go away…

          The sound of insects drowns out KINSEY and MR. X.

          CLARA, exhausted, pulls herself together as the drone of insects fades to silence.

CLARA: A 1938 survey published by the American Psychiatric Association revealed that women who reached orgasm easily had a peculiar dislike of pet canaries. I read this, and shared it with Prok, because, again, I thought it was funny. He didn't laugh. But he did say he'd look into it.

          CLARA retrieves The Book volume II from the crate beside her rocker and begins to leaf through it. MR. X has retrieved a copy of The Book volume II as well.

KINSEY: Sorry I'm late, Dr. Wolfe.

MR. X: That's quite alright. I've been keeping myself entertained with the new volume. I dare say it's more comprehensive than the first one.

KINSEY: I'm disappointed in the sales.

MR. X: It's only been out a couple of weeks. The first one took months to catch on.

KINSEY: Yes, and then it outsold Darwin. You'd think that would provide a bit of momentum. Did you see that piece of tripe they called a review in *The Journal*? It was the most pernicious, morally motivated garbage I've ever read. They should be ashamed, calling themselves scientists.

MR. X: Prok, it's eight hundred pages of technical jargon that no layman could possibly make sense of, it's prohibitively expensive, it's a singularly uninspired title—*Sexual Behavior in the Human Female*—it sounds about as exciting as a rash, and it's still sold over two hundred thousand copies in less than three weeks. And you're disappointed.

KINSEY: We need the money.

               Silence.

MR. X: I talked to the Rockefeller Foundation this morning.

KINSEY: And...

MR. X: All you have to do is play the game. They don't want the controversy. So let them keep you at arms length. What does it hurt, as long as the funding keeps coming?

KINSEY: This is about McCarthy, isn't it.

MR. X: I'll take care of that.

KINSEY: Why even dignify them with a response. Ignore it.

MR. X: They're not to be taken lightly. McCarthy's got the whole country running scared, and he and his little nest of henchmen are exactly who we don't want snooping around here right now.

KINSEY: Why? What are we afraid of? That they might find our gilded copy of the communist manifesto?

MR. X: Believe me, it's not something / we should...

KINSEY: / Oh come on, Arnold. They're accusing us of destroying the morals of western civilization, of making our country vulnerable to invasion by "The Red Menace." That book, that book you are holding in your hand right now is apparently more powerful than an atomic bomb, than an entire army. That book, which, by the way, does nothing more than quantify and report the sexual activities of people like McCarthy, is in actuality the instrument of our destruction. And I'm supposed to take that seriously.

MR. X: I will deal with it, alright? You don't need to concern yourself with them. It's the Foundation you need to worry about.

KINSEY: I've always held the Rockefeller in the highest regard.

MR. X: Our funding is coming from the National Research Council. Not directly from the Rockefeller. You know this. Yet not once, not in one of the hundreds of interviews you've done, have you made that clear.

KINSEY: I never felt that it required clarification. Besides, you know the press. They'll say what they want.

MR. X: I see what you do. You orchestrate the media like so many puppets. You enjoy the prestige of being associated directly with the Rockefeller, so that is the image you project, and they take their cues.

KINSEY: It's the most important and ground breaking research going on in the country right now. Possibly the world. Why shouldn't it be associated with the most important and prestigious funding body. And it's the truth. The Rockefeller funds the NRC, who in turn fund us. I don't see the harm in cutting out the middleman.

MR. X: The harm is we're going to lose our funding, and if we lose our funding the research will stop, and dozens of people will lose their jobs, and all of this will come to nothing. Because of your pride. We're obligated by letter to identify our primary funding source as the NRC. You're in breach of contract. I could fire you for what you're doing.

KINSEY: So fire me.

Silence.

Go ahead.

MR. X: I'm worried about you, Al. You're not invincible, but you keep pretending you are. Or maybe you believe it. But I'm telling you, as a friend, it's not true. You're human, just like the rest of us. Don't forget that.

KINSEY: Thank you for your concern. I mean that. Thank you. Do I still have a job?

MR. X: Of course you do.

KINSEY: I'll try to remember the NRC in my next interview.

MR. X: Thank you.

CLARA, in her rocker, has been watching KINSEY and MR. X.

KINSEY leaves MR. X, approaches CLARA.

KINSEY: I'll be off in short order. I can't imagine being more than a few days.

CLARA: Is David going with you?

KINSEY: No, he's staying behind this time. There's more than enough to keep him busy at the Institute.

CLARA: I'll check in on him, see if I can give him a hand.

KINSEY: Are you attracted to him?

              Silence.

              Are you?

CLARA: He's an attractive man.

KINSEY: I'm quite sure he's attracted to you, too. He's inferred as much.

              Silence.

              It wouldn't bother me.

CLARA: I wouldn't feel comfortable.

KINSEY: Why not?

CLARA: I know how you feel about him.

KINSEY: I have no particular feelings for David. You should explore the possibility.

CLARA: I'll have a think about it.

KINSEY: Mac. I want you to. I want you to be happy.

CLARA: Al...

KINSEY: Please.

              Silence.

CLARA: I'll have a think about it.

              KINSEY watches her for a moment, and then goes to his lecture position, addressing the audience.

KINSEY: I'll give you an example of the practical application of field work. All the medical literature up to the present maintains that fertilization of the egg depends on the squirting of semen into the cervix, yet the majority of the men I'd interviewed said that their semen dribbled rather than squirted upon ejaculation, so how could that be?

So, I enlisted the help of a young German prostitute, a very bright fellow who I'd been interviewing, he was only nineteen and he'd organized most of the trade on 42nd street and Bryant Park at the time, he knew everyone in the area.

MR. X approaches. KINSEY glances at him, but still addresses the audience.

I told him I needed to film as many men as possible masturbating to climax. I agreed to pay everyone who participated two dollars, and to give him one dollar for every person he brought in, and an additional fee for the use of his place.

CLARA has fished another document from the crate. She picks up the narrative, quietly amused by the experiment. KINSEY and MR. X have now locked on to each other, another contest of wills.

CLARA: "When the night for the filming arrived, the young man and I looked out his front window and saw a line that stretched all the way around the block. He became distressed as to what might happen to his rug, and proceeded to cover it with a large sheet, and before the end of the night he had to put a second one down. The data from the filming showed that the vast majority of the men, over 70 percent, dribbled rather than squirted, just as I had predicted, so fertilization, therefore, could not possible depend on the semen squirting into the cervix."

(To the audience.) And science marches on.

She returns her attention to the document. The fun she was having very quickly fades.

"It was later on that evening that the study took a most interesting turn. The young man had volunteered to show me how he could...how he could insert an object into his penis. He tied a rope around his scrotum, and pulled it tight, to keep himself erect, and then he used a toothbrush, the bristled end. He let us film it, but only from the waist down. I could see that he was having some difficulty, and...being familiar with the technique...I showed him how to bypass the tiny flap of skin partly up the urethra..."

CLARA stops reading.

MR. X: *(To KINSEY.)* You fell in love with him.

KINSEY: Who.

MR. X: The prostitute. From your lecture this afternoon.

KINSEY: I didn't realize you'd attended my lecture this afternoon, Mr. Lawrence.

MR. X: You fell in love with him, didn't you.

KINSEY: Why would you say that.

MR. X: He sounded like your type.

              Silence.

              It's okay. Everybody falls in love.

KINSEY: You're mistaken. I'd grown fond of him, but our relationship was based on his profession, and the information it provided for my studies.

MR. X: What a shame, really. That it should all be okay, any kind of shenanigans a body can get up to, it's all okay by you. As long as it's not genuine affection. As long as it's not love.

KINSEY: I don't think you should presume to know me so well.

MR. X: There are two kinds of people, Doc. The ones who fall in love and can handle it, and the one's who fall in love and can't. It's too bad, really, the ones like you. A life without love is hardly worth living, is it?

                I think that'll be enough for today.

                MR. X disengages, leaves the scene. CLARA returns the document to the crate, and goes and sets herself up to look at slides.

                Slide image: black and white. An adult couple, fucking. The slide is pornographic. There is nothing clinical about it.

CLARA: (*Addressing the audience.*) Prok lost interest in me, physically. We never stopped being intimate with one other. There was always intimacy. But intimacy doesn't always translate into sex, and if I learned anything from Prok's work I learned that sex is good. It's healthy. We should all have it. Lots of it.

                When he asked me to take up with David, I didn't have the heart to tell him I already had.

                Slide image: black and white. Discipline.

                Slide image: black and white. Bondage.

                Slide image: black and white. Sadomasochism.

                KINSEY approaches.

KINSEY: What are you doing?

                CLARA rubs her eyes, turns off the projector.

CLARA: Just browsing. How was Chicago?

KINSEY: Very productive. I secured over a hundred interviews.

CLARA: Mr. Lawrence called. He wants to add to his history again.

KINSEY stops. He is having minor pain in his leg.

Are you alright?

KINSEY: Yes, yes, fine. I'm just a little tired from the trip. Are you familiar with his file? Fascinating case. As a boy, he was abused by his grandmother and his father. All told he had sexual contact with seventeen of his relatives by the time he had reached adulthood. He's a walking id with polymorphous erotic tastes—sadomasochism, pedophilia, / bestiality…

CLARA: / He should be turned in.

I've been witness to a lot of very disturbing behavior over the last twenty years, Prok, but nothing like him. You can't let it go on. It's criminal.

KINSEY: Much of the behavior we study here is criminal. You know where I stand on this.

CLARA: They're children.

KINSEY: Why would you think that I'm not aware of that? Why would you think that I'm not sickened to my very core by the depravity of what he does? It disgusts me!

I am a scientist. I observe. The value of my work is in reflecting behavior, not changing it. There is no grey area. There can't be. There's too much at stake.

CLARA: What. What's at stake. Pie charts? Graphs? Pieces of paper? It's ink on a page. You pry into peoples' closets, you extract every dark little secret, and then you turn them into a number and stick them in a category. You talk to pedophiles and then dutifully tabulate occurrence ratios as if you were doing your taxes. And you would interview the children, too, if you had the opportunity. Wouldn't you?

It's hypocrisy, Al. We're drowning in our own hypocrisy. We hide behind this cloak of objective reason, as if the holy grail of science grants us some special immunity, some higher power that lifts us up out of the filth, and depravity. But it's a lie.

KINSEY: I know / it's hard.

CLARA: / It's a lie, / Prok.

KINSEY: / I know it's hard. I know that. I do feel things, Clara.

I also know, deeply, completely, that we are doing something good here. We're seeking the truth. I trust that.

CLARA: You're not going to save the world by allowing him to go free, Prok. It's a lie. A trick of the mind. You've been living it for so long that you think it's the truth. You've convinced yourself that you're above it all, separate from it, untouchable. But you aren't. You're in it. We all are. We're all part of it. And I don't know if I can do it anymore.

             Silence.

I'm in love with David.

I'm sorry.

             She leaves KINSEY, and returns to the garden. She gathers herself, addressing the audience, occasionally looking at KINSEY, taking him in.

CLARA: There's a particular plant, a weed, that took over most of Prok's garden. Yarrow. Achillea Millefolium. In the language of flowers, Yarrow is called the herb of the Devil, and means war. The roots of this particular weed seek out other plants' roots, and once they have found them, they grow along side them and emerge through the soil where the other plant has already broken through.

KINSEY has returned to the loose floorboard. He retrieves the worn toothbrush, examines it.

It so entwines itself with the root system of the host plant that to get rid of it you have to get rid of everything. Everything must be pulled up. Everything must die. And even at that, there will be some seed that lies dormant, or some piece of root too deep, beyond your reach. Once it has found its way into your garden, you must remain diligent for the rest of your life. If you don't, it will take advantage. It will quickly and mercilessly reclaim everything that you worked so hard to win back.

CLARA watches KINSEY return the toothbrush to its hiding place.

Love is a selfish act. It's not about caring, or giving. There's nothing grand or noble about it. We fall in love because we need. Because we are afraid. We fall in love with the person who makes us feel the least alone. That's all love is.

The sound of insects builds in. MR. X's voice merges with the sound of the insects, / taking it over.

MR. X: / Come here, go away, come here, go away, come here, go away. It always comes to that. That's when you can tell they're ready. That's when you know they want it. They keep saying no but their bodies begin to co-operate, to open up, they invite you, and tell you where to go, and what to do. This one got wet, it felt good, the lube…

KINSEY: Did you fuck her or use your fingers?

*MR. X is looking at KINSEY, studying him.
KINSEY is exhausted, fighting for focus. CLARA
watches.*

MR. X: I used my fingers. I tried to fuck her, but I couldn't
                stay hard.

KINSEY: Did you come?

MR. X: I jerked myself off while I rubbed her. I took her for
                ice cream after. She had strawberry.

KINSEY: How did you feel afterwards, Mr. Lawrence?

MR. X: What do you mean?

KINSEY: After she left you. How did you feel.

MR. X: I felt fine. How does it feel when you suck a cock?

KINSEY: Pardon me?

MR. X: Your turn. Tell me how you feel when you have a
                cock in your mouth.

KINSEY: I'm not providing the history, Mr. Lawrence, you
                are. You say you felt fine. What does that mean?
                What were you thinking / about?

MR. X: / No. Tell me what it feels like.

KINSEY: I would have no way of knowing.

MR. X: Lie.

                Silence.

KINSEY: I think that will be enough for today. Please feel
                free to call if you'd like to contribute further.

MR. X: You like to hurt yourself. Don't you?

                I know who you are, Doc. I know all about you. I've
                read your books, your papers, done my
                homework. I've been following your interviews,
                too. I've heard you talk about me.

KINSEY: That's not possible. All histories are strictly confidential. You know that.

MR. X: I see myself. You can't hide me. I'm in all the numbers.

KINSEY: I can assure you, there is no / possible way that you...

MR. X: / It's okay. I don't mind. I like it. Being the star. We're not that different, you know. You and me. We're both looking for something to pull us out, make us feel alive. Wake us up. I can smell it on you. You're stuck inside yourself. Buried. Scared shitless. What does it take to get you out of there, Doc? To get you back in your body? A little pain? Hmm? A little twist? A little tug, a little / pinch...

KINSEY: / What is it you're trying to do, Mr. Lawrence? Are you trying to get a rise out of me? Is that what you're attempting? Because it won't work. Even if I had engaged in homosexual behavior, there is absolutely no correlation between that and masochism. Your inference carries no statistical weight.

MR. X: I like it when you squirm. It makes me hard. I'd like to watch you sometime. When you do it. When you hurt yourself.

KINSEY: Good day, Mr. Lawrence.

KINSEY starts to leave.

MR. X: Do you count yourself? In all your numbers and scribbles there, do you count yourself? Where do you fit in?

Just curious.

KINSEY: I'll be closing your file, Mr. Lawrence. This will be our last interview. Thank you for your time.

MR. X has taken KINSEY's place at his desk.

MR. X: How about I plan something special for you. Maybe sisters. I haven't done sisters before. What do you say. A couple of sisters for the stats?

The sound of insects begins to build.

Oh come on. Don't get all bent out of shape. I'm doing it for you. It's a gift. You and me, we're going to have the whole world watching, my friend. We're going to change the whole world. So what do you think, sisters? Or maybe something really young. How young do you think I can get? Something really young and sweet and sassy, all come here go away come here go away come here go away…

The sound of insects is deafening, drowning out MR. X.

KINSEY is gripped by a sharp pain in his leg, buckling him. CLARA watches.

The sound of insects recedes, fading under the following. KINSEY is isolated by a bright, redemptive light, alone. He looks at CLARA, taking her in.

KINSEY: It was the end of my first year of university. I was studying biology, and I was walking across the campus, delivering a box of text books for a professor, as a favour. It was an unusually warm spring day, and I took my shoes off, and the weight of the text books pushed down through my body, driving my winter soft bare feet into the sharp stones and tiny bits of shiny glass imbedded in the hot cement of the sidewalk. I was aware of the pain, but it didn't stop me. I began to fall into my step, pounding my feet down into the sidewalk, a soldier marching to a rhythm deep inside my bones, deep inside my flesh, a rhythm that I did not know I had. The pain shooting up through the soles of my feet releases me, and the past falls away, and there is no future, and I can't remember how old I am, or how young, and I am beyond definition, beyond expectation, and for the very first time in my life I simply exist, here, in this moment. I forget to think, and I forget to reason, and I simply am. I simply am. I am. I am. I am. I am. I am.

Silence.

Birdsong. A slow, warm summer day.

KINSEY approaches CLARA. He sits.

CLARA glances at KINSEY, taking his measure.

CLARA: Beautiful day.

KINSEY: What time is it?

CLARA: Two-ish. Are you alright?

KINSEY: We lost our funding.

CLARA: Oh, Alfred. I'm sorry.

KINSEY: It got away from me. I lost sight of what I was trying to do. I wrote everything down, everything, except that.

        KINSEY looks at CLARA, lost, searching.

        I don't know what part of it is real anymore, Mac. What part of it is real life, and what part is made up.

CLARA: Real life is right here, sweetheart. This lovely day, and the sun shining, and the birds singing. It's right in front of you. It's right here.

        A long silence. KINSEY looks away.

KINSEY: I'm going to do some work in the garden.

We hear one of KINSEY's classical pieces.

CLARA watches as KINSEY makes his way into the overgrown garden, and begins working. A pain in his leg grips him, and he falls to the ground. His light fades to black.

The music fades. We hear birds singing, a return of the gentle buzz of insects, comforting, hot and lazy.

CLARA gets up and goes to her corner of the garden, and begins to weed.

MR. X enters, watches her.

MR. X: You've got your work cut out for you.

CLARA: Jesus. David. You scared the shit out of me.

MR. X: Sorry. Just thought I'd drop by. I never got much of a chance to talk to you at the funeral.

CLARA: Can I get you anything? I've made some lemonade.

MR. X: No, thank you. I have to get back to the Institute. We have a grant hearing this afternoon.

CLARA: Do you think the place will survive?

MR. X: I don't know. I'm going to do my best.

CLARA: You're a smart man. I'm sure you'll do just fine.

MR. X: *(Referring to the garden.)* Looks like a big job.

CLARA: I'm just going after this little corner here. To start with, anyway. Put down some tomatoes.

MR. X: It's a good time for it. The bugs have all but disappeared.

CLARA: Yes. It's strange. A blessing, I suppose.

They catch each other's eye. A moment. CLARA looks away.

MR. X: The medical report said it was a clot?

CLARA: He fell in the garden and bruised his knee. They think the bruising released an embolism, and it went up to his heart. He was a sickly child. He never did have a very strong heart. And there were infections, other problems. He wasn't in good health.

Silence.

I don't think I can see you anymore, David. When I look at you, I see him. When I think of you and I together, he's there. That's not how I want to remember him. I'm sorry.

Silence.

I'd still like to be your friend.

MR. X: I understand.

Have a fine day, Clara.

CLARA: You as well.

MR. X leaves. CLARA watches after him. She considers, and then goes to KINSEY's desk and retrieves the picture of Victor. She takes the picture and puts it away in the crate beside her rocker. She addresses the audience, as she returns to her garden.

That weed, Yarrow. Some people don't think of it as a weed. They treat it like a flower. Something desirable, and useful. Prok used it for contrast, a backdrop for all the showy blooms upfront.

I might keep a wee patch of it, off in the corner there. Give the garden a bit of an edge, something that needs to be watched, something a little dangerous. Prok would have liked that. And if it gets away from me, if it takes over all the other flowers and I have to rip it all up again, that's alright. I'll reclaim the best plants, my favourites, the ones I remember as being the most hardy, and the most beautiful, and I'll plant it all again. It's my garden now. I can do that.

Prok died on Sunday, August 25th, 1956. He was 62 years old.

A short time after his death, a young couple arrived on my doorstep. It was two men, but I knew instantly that they were a couple. They were comfortable with each other, at ease. They were themselves. I thought they were curiosity seekers. Come to gawk at the widow of the infamous Alfred C. Kinsey. I get a lot of that. But they'd come to pay homage. They believed that they would not have been able to accept themselves, and each other, as normal, if Alfred hadn't started that dialogue, if he hadn't opened that door of perception. They loved each other, and they wanted to thank him for that.

I would have liked very much for him to have met that couple. I think it would have made him very happy.

She takes in the garden.

The sound of birds singing.

CLARA goes back to her reclamation.

Lights fade to black.

The End.